Lauren
Grantham

ry

ρ/1-07

JUL 2006

A2032 4653729

Copyright © 2006 Dr. D. Hann Morrison, Ph. D, LPC
All rights reserved.
ISBN: 1-4196-3121-7

To order additional copies, please contact us.
BookSurge, LLC
www.booksurge.com
1-866-308-6235
orders@booksurge.com

DR. D. HANN MORRISON, Ph. D, LPC

EVEN SUPERWOMAN NEEDS TO CRY SOMETIMES

An Intimacy Guide For Men Partnering With Strong Black Women

2006

Even Superwoman Needs To Cry Sometimes

TABLE OF CONTENTS

Foreword	xv
Introduction	xix
Chapter I: SBW????	1
Chapter II: 'Ain't I A Woman'…	9
Chapter III: The Education of the Black Woman	15
Chapter IV: "…she can do it all, and all by herself; she doesn't need me."	29
Chapter V: "So, How Do I Partner with the SBW?"	35
1) Get to know her	41
2) Develop an appreciation for who she is	45
3) Support her interests	49
4) Approach the relationship as a partnership	53
5) Spend time working on yourself	65
Working on Self From The Inside Out	69
5a) Introspection	71
5b) Ownership.	75
5c) Facing your fears	79
Chapter VI: A Final Word To The Strong Black Woman	81
Afterword	89

ABOUT THE BOOK

Even Superwoman Needs To Cry Sometimes…is a frank look at the emotional needs of the Strong Black Woman (SBW)—that under the tough persona is a spirit that needs nurturing. The book speaks to how the notion of Black women's "toughness" has become encompassing, while looking intensely at how this notion has adversely impacted intimate relationships between African American men and women. In addition to looking at the historical roots of the conceptualization of the SBW, consideration is given to current trends that continually perpetuate this widespread notion. The book offers those involved in intimate relationships with African American women basic principles for focusing on the relationship and the emotional needs of the strong Black woman (SBW).

ACKNOWLEDGMENTS

I must first acknowledge and thank our Father Who art in heaven...Who has so generously blessed my life. Not the least of these blessings being the interest in, and aptitude for written expression;

Sincere thanks goes out to my network of family, friends, and colleagues who had faith in me and my ability to provide effective discourse on such a sensitive topic. Thank you for you unwavering faith in me even when I, myself, found my faith waning;

I'd like to especially thank my manuscript readers
Sara Hann Perkins
Dr. Jack Shortridge
Dr. Robert M. Knight
Roger McMillan
Major Donna McNabb

*This Book Is Dedicated To The People Whose Love
Sustains Me Most—
My Grandchildren,
Allyn Grace Mcguire
And
Shawn Andrew (Scooter) Mcguire,
And Their Parents,
Shawn And Randi Mcguire
And My Mother
Mrs. Gertrude Townsend Hann*

FOREWORD

In Strong Black Woman, Dee Morrison has written a notably revealing book, in which she discusses the difficulties in developing healthy, intimate personal relationships between African-American men and women, where the woman is, in fact—like Dr. Morrison herself—a Strong Black Woman.

Written, clearly, from the author's perspective—one shared, as she suggests, by other highly accomplished African-American women—Dr. Morrison explores various social, cultural and psychological dynamics which she, and others, have faced in their relationships with men. Often men not nearly as accomplished (in comparable ways) to their female counterparts.

As a non-African American male, I would see many of these same dynamics applicable, as well, in non-African American male-female personal relationships. For example, I've already referred to such relationships at least twice, so far, and both times I have put the male ahead of the female (in what I've written). As if that isn't "the way it is"—from a typical male perspective—African-American or not. Indeed, over the years, I have often asked the African-American women I've taught in graduate school, which they've experienced more of: racism or sexism? In recent years, it seems that more of the women have reported having to deal more often with racism; while in years past, I think I heard more, proportionately, describing sexism as more oppressive.

In this book Dr. Morrison describes, as common, a lack of sensitivity (on the part of black males) to the emotional needs of black females (even—perhaps especially—the Strong Black Woman). Her point being, that eventhough such women may be highly accomplished—educationally, professionally, or otherwise—even such achievement: it nonetheless fails to address the deeper, more sensitive (and certainly) more vulnerable emotional needs of such accomplished women.

It is here, I think, that Dr. Morrison has put her finger on something as significant as it is problematic. The fact that highly accomplished people—including the Strong Black Woman—that such folk are often over-developed in ways that promote achievement (educationally and professionally, for instance), yet are just as under-developed in owning their vulnerability and sensitivity in more personal, intimate relationships. If the Strong Black Woman may be quite accomplished in "taking care of herself"—not to mention, providing care to and for others—she may find it just as difficult, perhaps even threatening, to receive care and nurture. Even from a "Strong Black Man"; much less, a seemingly "Weak Black Man." Assuming such men are, in fact, capable of providing reciprocal nurture and care, which Dr. Morrison describes as not often being the case. As though such vulnerability somehow betrays an apparent lack of strength, competence and control. And, of course—as I've suggested—this problem is hardly unique to the Strong Black Woman, as unique as the circumstances of the Strong Black Woman may be.

Any relationship—and certainly, an intimate female-male personal relationship—will always be characterized, in some way or other, by the relative emotional strength of the persons involved. In other words, when either person tends to so over-power the other, the consequences are usually problematic. However, I have known couples where the woman was clearly smarter, better educated, more accomplished (and even made more money) than her male counterpart: yet neither seemed to be threatened by this apparent inequity (at the social level), because—at an emotional level—such a power differential seemed not to exist between the two. What Dee Morrison describes, however, is quite the opposite: a chronic social-psychological syndrome, in which too many of the men they encounter appear to be perhaps even intimidated by the Strong Black Woman, and consequently relate in maladaptive ways.

I've known Dr. Morrison, for a number of years, in a variety of roles: as a student, as a supervisee, and as a professional colleague (in teaching and consulting). I admire, respect and value her greatly. I also like her; she's my friend. Indeed, I hold Dee Morrison in the highest personal and professional regard, and I commend to you her book, Strong Black Woman.

The Reverend Robert M. Knight, D. Min.

INTRODUCTION

Even Superwoman Needs To Cry Sometimes...is the result of the collaboration of at least three forces—clinical practice; intellectual undertakings; and real life (my own). Throughout my life I'd seen a stark discrepancy between the emotional treatment and expectations of African American women and white women. Living in the south made the differences all the more pronounced, as the gentile southern lady persona served as a backdrop of all the African American woman was not. While white women were afforded a broad range of options for the expression of emotions, their Black counterparts were not. African American women were expected to "hold it together" at all times. We weren't supposed to cry or express tenderness or a need for tenderness. Funerals were the one exception. (I now often wonder if this is the reason, or at least one of the reasons, anyway, why African American funerals were usually such high context affairs, with lots of keening, wailing, and a variety of emotional shenanigans). We were supposed to be tough—all the time; no matter what.

In clinical practice as well as in the classroom (graduate, as well as undergraduate) I've borne witness to women who were frazzled (for lack of any better word to describe their horrific state of burn-out), but who couldn't seem to garner the support or understanding for their condition from either family or employer. Both bosses and husbands seem oblivious to these women's plights, as they juggled school, overwhelming work responsibilities, children, spouses, household duties, and community work. These women often come to counseling with years of pent up resentment, emotional exhaustion, and teetering on the brink of insanity. All they want, I've learned, is just permission to take off that damn cape and exhale; they want to be relieved of the responsibility for just a bit; they want the opportunity to be hysterical if they choose; to cry sometimes; to be a woman. While this book speaks primarily to the issues facing the strong Black woman (SBW), I feel it important to note at this juncture, that the aforementioned experiences are not necessarily exclusive to SBW, but also, in many instances, to the professional Black man. In fact, an articulate professional male colleague of mine, whose opinions I value highly, put it to me this way: "Women have each other to cry to and with; who can a Black man express himself with and still feel comfortable the next time they meet?" This gentleman observed, rather accurately, that fewer and fewer African American males are pursuing higher education, making it difficult, in his opinion, to find a peer with whom the professional Black male can relate on a level beyond sports or other superficial lines of conversations. My friend and colleague shared that, like his female counterpart, the Black male professional also wants a safe environment that would allow him to shed the superman cape. One major difference he contends, is that the male doesn't have the option of crying. In his words, if the Black man sheds a tear in the presence of his intimate female partner or in the presence of his street-tough male buddies, he will have compromised his place in the relationship—he would then be considered weak, the recovery from which, he says, is almost impossible.

It is not the contention of this book to deny or otherwise refute the social and emotional challenges faced by the African American male in pursuit of higher levels of professional development. It is unfortunate that anyone (either male or female) would be emotionally penalized for professional growth, but it is fortunate that this forum is presented as a mechanism to develop sensitivity to one another's plight and to get about the business of healing.

As I and my female colleagues rose to greater academic and professional heights, I began to see marriages all around me falling apart for what seemed like little or no reason at all. Women in the classroom have been generous in sharing that their pursuit of educational and professional advancement have left them wanting and needing even greater understanding and support from the home front. Paradoxically though, they, at this crucial time in their lives, discovered that they've had to fend for themselves, all by themselves. I found that their stories were almost identical to those of the women I saw in the practice setting. The primary difference between the accounts of the students in the classroom and the accounts I heard in the counseling session was that in the clinical arena these women had usually been, or were on their way, to divorce court. The intimate relationships of women still pursuing their degrees were in trouble, but hadn't totally fallen apart. Having earned the degree, however, seems to have been positively correlated with divorce or separation. Women were leaving their graduate school commencements and heading straight to the courthouse. They are waving newly earned degrees in one hand, while clutching their divorce decrees in the other. The victory was bittersweet. What had she gained if she'd lost all that was important? Was this the price for success? Husbands were anguished by wives who had outgrown them, while wives were mourning relationships they had counted on as long term investments.

I have had the opportunity to see a few couples dealing with the issue of the assault to the male's definition of his place in the relationship when his wife/partner is considered to be a strong black woman. While the initial presentations are sometimes different, over time, however, the underlying issues are dangerously similar—she's smart; she's tough; she's assertive in her professional life and the man in intimate partnership with her cannot separate his wife's personal life from her professional life. The outcomes have not been positive. The dissolution and decline of marriage among African Americans has now far exceeded the national average. According to the U. S. Census Bureau, African American married couples are at considerably higher risk for divorce than other ethnic groups. This is not to be construed as a cultural devaluation of marriage, but just that the complexities of married life become too overwhelming for couples to sustain. Of even greater concern is the fact that African American women who divorce have a lower than average probability of re-marriage compared to divorced women of other ethnic groups.

The frequency with which I saw this issue professionally, academically, and personally served as a potent indicator that discourse on the topic was warranted. Events in my own life then led me to know, with certainty, that this topic was in need of treatment. I pondered for some time how and to whom I should present this discussion. I initially thought to target those thought of as SBW. After all, I reasoned, they would certainly be able to identify with the issues. I had no doubt that the SBW would be a much more receptive audience, at least in terms of being amenable to hearing/reading, internalizing and applying the concepts this contribution puts forth. But then I discerned that merely identifying with the issue was not my true intent. Rather, enlightenment regarding the issue was at least one of the goals I wanted to accomplish. I realized, further, that acknowledgment and validation of accompanying feelings and reactions to the issue were also important in this undertaking. And finally, I was certain that my goal in producing this book included not just enlightenment on the issue, but most importantly, providing mechanisms to mediate the issue. These were the lessons I wanted to teach. After some reflection I thought better of the notion to target SBW. I thought it much more prudent to share these insights with the men and/or other women who partner intimately with SBW. After reflection on my clinical and personal experiences it seemed to make greater sense that the partners of SBW would benefit more immediately and more profoundly from the information herein.

Strangely enough, it seems that the male intimate partners of SBW's had bought intensely into the myth that their women could actually 'do it all', and without them. They seem, based on my clinical and academic observations, to have erroneously adopted as truth the notion that because their spouses had overcome the racial and gender hurdles that would ordinarily bar them from fulfilling careers, that somehow their wives had all they'd ever wanted or needed. These men seem to have forgotten all about their partners' humanness and their human need for caring, for nurturing, and for intimately belonging.

The issues undertaken in this contribution are

not without considerable depth and breadth in African American culture. I suspect, in fact, that much of the discussion might well apply to relationships across racial, cultural or sexual orientation lines. Because of my clinical, academic, and personal experience, however, I will speak primarily to the African American male-female intimate relationship. I acknowledge wholeheartedly that perspectives on this topic are, and will be, as varied as human beings, themselves, and could easily take up great volumes of text. My goal for this book was, and continues to be, that it be concise and easily readable; that it bring enlightenment without burdening the reader with copious academic discourse. My goal is that this book become the catalyst for dialogue at every conceivable level. Therefore, I strived arduously to make this book short and to the point. Most of us are not intensely interested in a lot of theoretical notions, we just want to know what works for us—what can bring us to our goals—- and what is simple, what is achievable, and what is practical. I hope this book brings great insight to couples and individuals everywhere. It is a book that can and should be read over and over again—it should serve as a reference for couples and individuals, alike. Every person currently in or considering an intimate partnership with a women he or she describes as a strong black woman should own this book.

-1-
SBW ???????

EVEN SUPERWOMAN NEEDS TO CRY SOMETIMES

SBW—ugh! What started out as supposedly a compliment to our resiliency and ability to overcome obstacles in pursuit of professional development and just basic everyday survival has turned into a curse of sorts. The initials alone, have become an insult that some Black women, especially, professional women, have come to abhor with great passion. Books have been written about her; corporate America embraces her as the source of getting done what seemed impossible; white men see her as the pink bunny in the battery commercial "…. that just keeps going and going"; her family is proud of her; black men are in awe of her, but at the same time seem to be intimidated by her; and other women just see her as incredible. The Strong Black Woman (SBW)—the epitome of perseverance and discipline. A good thing…by most accounts. Throughout the text I will use the initials 'SBW' to refer to African American women who have been decisive regarding their personal and professional growth. These women have worked or are working diligently to make their futures great in spite of their pasts. These women do not fear success and they certainly do not fear failure. Some, I suspect have at least a time or two in the quest for greatness in their respective fields, but have gotten up, brushed off and rejoined the race with renewed commitment and determination. These women do not make excuses—the circumstances of neither history, race, nor gender have stood in the way of their pursuit of educational and professional growth.

Neither superman, nor his modern middle class American counterpart, Supermom, has anything on this phenomenal woman—she (metaphorically, at least) leaps tall buildings in a single bound, but has to do it twice as fast; she doesn't just stop speeding bullets, but must do so with her left hand, as her right hand is busy turning the pages of the book she's reading as she maneuvers through Atlanta traffic at 6:45 in the morning. She knows she must pay the Black Tax. The determination and charisma these women exude are too often inaccurately perceived as callus recklessness or aggressiveness in the pursuit of the almighty dollar. Not so. These are women who are talented in their respective fields. They come armed with creativity, wisdom, wit, intelligence, and other traits that are assigned positive value in males or white females. She's had to struggle for validation because of the amount of melanin in her skin.

Without question, African American women have come a long way with regard to their educational and professional attainment. According to the Bureau of Labor Statistics, white collar African American women are currently the next to the highest wage earners in this country. Positioning themselves next to white males in earning potential is the result of significantly greater educational achievement than white women or black men, and a demonstrated capacity to "get the job done". African American women are serious about their careers and have established a reputation of productivity, excellence and quality in their chosen fields. This upward movement, although, economically, professionally, and egotistically rewarding, has meant, for some, however, a movement not just up, but rather 'out'. Upward mobility of African American women is positively correlated with challenges to social and familial adjustment of these women. Moving up, for many, has meant moving from a place of social and geographical comfort and acceptance to a place where their identities as Black women may be seen as tenuous, at best. These women may struggle with issues of acceptance in the workplace as well as in their communities. Some may be accused of having forgotten their roots, while others experience an all-out assault to their personhood. Any display of her economic prowess, and the SBW's femininity is questioned; indulgence of her taste for the finer things in life makes her less than Black.

While the SBW is seen as an icon of sorts, she is also representative of a growing number of women whose lives have become void of intimacy. She is seen as strong and able to overcome all obstacles. She is viewed by contemporaries and by her community as having it all together. She is also seen as having absolutely no need. Whether or not these perceptions are based in some fragment of fact, are purely myth or somewhere in between is debatable. What isn't left to debate, however, is the fact that these same perceptions will become issues that warrant mediation in the personal lives of SBW. Whether she's negotiating a multi-billion dollar business merger, testifying before a domestic violence senate subcommittee on Capital Hill, operating a back-hoe on a road improvement project, or changing diapers at a day care, the Black woman is still expected to function fully and with minimal support at home and in her community. The African American woman, by all accounts, has yet another full shift of housework, community work, or church work ahead of her after the five PM closing bell. What seems to go unnoticed, and therefore unattended, are her needs for familial support and emotional nurturing. What is most often missing in her life are outlets that will afford her full expression of the woman she is. The strong Black woman needs opportunities to cease being the rock of Gibraltar for at least some parts of her day.

For the man in her life, the SBW's persona can be deceiving. She appears to have it all under control. She just keeps taking on more and appears to need him less. She seems to have all this energy, and people rely on her far more than she relies on others. It is not uncommon for him to become confused about the value of his role in her life. From what he can tell, she can do it all, and all by herself. In his view, the more she rises, the more he wanes. As she grows, he seems to pale. All he can see is how incredibly powerful she has become and how his power, as a spouse, as a provider, and as a man seems to dissipate before his eyes. Are his feelings valid, or are they the product of a male ego bruised by insecurity? Is this an issue of personal insecurity, or a true cultural phenomenon? Is he just plain egotistical, or should he be legitimately fearful? Should he struggle against the tide of tradition to redefine his role in the relationship, or should he strive to preserve what's left of his manhood at the cost of the relationship when the prospect of having both seems bleak?

The next section of this book will address the historical origins of Black women's assumption of strength, stamina, and stoicism. We will then consider current educational trends that seem to perpetuate the problem. The book will culminate with five basic relationship principles that facilitate understanding and growth between SBW's and their intimate partners.

-2-
Ain't I a Woman

EVEN SUPERWOMAN NEEDS TO CRY SOMETIMES

Nobody ever helped her out of a buggy, or placed a coat over a mud puddle for her. On May 29th 1851 she boldly reminded a women's suffrage group in Akron, Ohio of the problem of the status of women in the United States. Sojourner Truth made a point, however, of delineating even then, the deference that was not accorded to women of color. Nearly a hundred years later, Langston Hughes' poem "The Negro Mother" was still describing the black woman as the person still not yet deserving of love, safety, or respect. The unfortunate fact is that society has long overlooked the need of the African American woman to be nurtured. While pampering, or simply according deference and respect was traditional and expected with regard to White women, African American women were not allowed such luxury. Rather, Black women were expected to take care of everybody else, even at the expense of her own needs. She was revered for her "toughness"—her ability to 'take a lick'in and keep on tick'in'. Crying was not an option for the African American woman; she was expected to master the art of sucking it up. And so, many, for the sake of survival, wore the suit of emotional armor and kept moving. By the time the Black woman had fed, clothed, cleaned after, and entertained literally dozens of children (her own as well as Miss Ann's); cleaned two houses (her own and Miss Ann's); and attended to the needs of her husband, as well as the demands made by Miss Ann's husband, there was not much left to her but sheer numbness. She was used, abused, tossed aside, and ignored. Little regard was given to her feelings. How ever she felt about all that was happening to her and around her was her's to deal with alone, quietly, and without expression. As a reader of history I can only imagine, although with great chagrin, the powerlessness that Black men must have felt bearing witness on a daily basis to wives, mothers, sisters and aunts being subjected to such a harsh existence. It would make sense then, for the black male to himself, develop a sense of numbness, so as not to become completely consumed with a condition over which he too, had little, if any control.

Most rational people would have to agree that the institution of slavery in America has left indelible marks on Black culture in this country—from our definition of ourselves to the basics of how or what we teach our children; from the way we interact with the White race, to how we interact with one another. Without minimizing the depth and magnitude of the lessons we learned from slavery, and certainly without suggesting that racism does not continue to exist in this country, I firmly promote the notion that it is time to create a new history. At least with regard to our interpersonal relationships. More specifically, I think its time (past time, actually) to rethink our conceptualization of the African American woman: who she is; what she is all about; her goals; her feelings; her role in our lives and in her own life. We would want to teach America how to treat African American women by demonstrating the value we place on our own. The validation and reverence of our own would need to start in our own communities; in our own households. The history we would want to create is one that demonstrates for our daughters that Black women are prized; that Black women are revered; that Black women are honored. This history that I propose we leave should be one that clearly shows African American girls that African American men recognize them as fully functioning human beings with needs that transcend the mere physical. We want to instruct them through our own behaviors, that their feelings are valid and should be validated at the very least, within their intimate relationships. Perhaps we would want our daughters to know that men of their race actually appreciate their skills, their talents, and their wholeness as women. We'd want them to know that Black males appreciate Black females' willingness to so openly give of themselves in relationships that propel us all forward emotionally, and otherwise. We want this new history because it will teach our daughters what to expect in healthy relationships. As a culture we want it for our sons because they will learn how to contribute to the health and productivity of interpersonal relationships and propagate generations of children who will not practice the subtle, but all the same, damaging forms of self hate.

I suggest a new paradigm that accords the Black woman the right, or the privilege, if you will, to be as feminine as she pleases; to be as vulnerable as she pleases; to think of her as deserving of love, safety, and respect. Believe it or not, Black women, regardless of how much money they earn, or what time they clock in or out of work, do want to be helped out of carriages. And no, it certainly would not hurt for men to occasionally lay down their coats to help the SBW negotiate a mud puddle.

-3-
The Education of the Black Woman

EVEN SUPERWOMAN NEEDS TO CRY SOMETIMES

Education, without a doubt, has been the catalyst that has propelled African Americans to economic heights that only a century ago were mere fantasy. As well it should, advances in educational levels within the Black community are responsible for exponential leaps in lifestyle changes that can be seen over a single generation. While no one questions the benefits of education, what is clearly an asset may be interpreted to be a major dividing factor within African American culture. Allow me to clarify that it is not education itself that is at issue. What is at issue, rather, is the educational disparity and the vastness of educational disparities between the genders in Black America that is a contributor to social decline in the African American community.The disparity between the educational attainment of African American women and African American men is nothing less that astounding. While African American girls earn high school diplomas at a higher rate than their male counterparts, the differences become increasingly more marked with higher levels of education. At the baccalaureate, graduate, and post graduate levels, the numbers tell an almost alarming story. African American girls enter and complete college at a much higher rate that African American boys. In 1993, for example, while African American females made up 11.1% of college enrollment in the United States, African American males made up 8.5%. That same year 226,000 more Black women than Black men graduated from college. According to the American Council on Education (ACE), women tend to be represented on college campuses more than males regardless of race, with the Black male-female educational attainment disparity being rather pronounced, as compared to other ethnic groups. The ACE reported that in a 20-year span (from 1980 to 2000) African American male college enrollment saw a 37% increase, rising from 464,000 to 635,000. For the same period however, African American females' college enrollment numbers rose from 643,000 to 1.1 million– a 70% increase. These figures constitute a difference of 450,000 more college enrolled Black women than Black men by the year 2000. The educational disparity between African American males and females is greater than that of other ethnic groups. The relative numbers of college enrollment between men and women of other races were not nearly as broad. Among Hispanics, for example, in 2000 there was a difference of about 200,000 more college enrolled females than males, with the difference in the Asian community being around 50,000. Additionally, the educational differentials between Black women and Black men at the levels of advanced degrees is even more stark. It is a documented fact that African American women pursue advanced degrees at a significantly higher rate than their male counterparts.

Simply put, African American women have achieved significantly greater heights in education, and consequently, in professional opportunities than Black males. This disparity in education translates, as it might well be expected to, into gross disparities in professional responsibilities, professional status, and earning potential between these two groups. These economic and social differences have become, it seems, a source of contention between Black men and women, when in actuality, it needn't necessarily be.

While most men are quick to voice their support, and delight of spouses who out-earn them, over time, however, and with continuous taunting from allegedly well-meaning friends the issue of salary differentials can become a threat to the stability of marital and other interpersonal relationships. A common description of his feeling by men who make it into therapy is that they feel 'dethroned' or 'trumped' by their wives. In addition to the financial issue, there may also arise social problems that go hand in hand with the issue of the higher educated-higher earning wife. With the depths of the educational differences between African American males and females deepening every day, it is not unreasonable to infer that African American women who marry within their race are almost certain to marry someone with considerably less education than she has. Even if he earns as much as she does, or out-earns her, for that matter, their social circles are usually quite different. Their repertoire of social responses and responsiveness and modalities for interpersonal interactions may be quite different. Social interactions with one another's friends and colleagues may be challenging at best, but in some cases downright difficult.

DR. D. HANN MORRISON, PH. D, LPC

Inconsistent with most men's perceptions, the Black woman's progress in her professional life is usually no indication of any intent or attempt to minimize the value of the Black male's role in the family. Contrary to media portrayal, African American families are generally patriarchal, with the male holding a role as a vital member of the parenting team. In very traditional African American households, in fact, the male has greater clout than his wife. The African American male's role as a spouse is no less important, regardless of his income, social or professional status, or level of educational attainment. He is an active contributor in the management of the household. He is no less than fifty percent of the decision-making team in matters of finances, child rearing, religion, and other major issues. The Black male continues to be viewed by his partner and children as the protector of the household and the nurturer of his partner's spirit.

Rather than as an affront to their partners, professional Black women tend to see their achievements as the culmination of years of hard work. African American women who pursued higher education have typically not had the luxury of foregoing full time employment while attending school. Even those undertaking the rigors of graduate education have generally had to learn to juggle the demands of work, household tasks, children, spouse, and school, all at the same time. Given the overwhelming challenges of pursing her professional dreams, it is no wonder then, that the reward of recognition for the Black woman's achievement takes on an air of sweetness. The economic rewards, they say, are merely a source from which their families may draw to ease the burdens on their spouses/partner and to facilitate greater leisure and quality for the family. African American women in dual income families tend to see their incomes as a supplement to their partners'. This is true even of those who earn considerably more than their spouses. These women do not wield inordinate power with regard to their contributions to the household finances.

Despite African American women's great achievements in education and rise to the board room, the fact remains that we continue to live in a race and gender oriented society. So, does the Black woman's rise to a position of great responsibility and visibility make her life easier? Some would be inclined to say a resounding "yes". However, when asked to remove economics as a component for consideration, most women overwhelmingly respond in the negative. Black women recognize rather openly that the movement to the top carries with it the additional burden of being scrutinized severely and criticized even more harshly than their White male or female peers. These women tend to describe their experiences as being under the microscope and/or of representing the entire race—a burden that is not only cumbersome, but wholly unfair. The tokenism and conformity that often comes with growth of this type can prove to be nothing less than overwhelming. Some women describe their experiences as that of having to arm themselves for battle every single day. These women have to prove themselves over and over again, while their credibility as contributing members of the work team is constantly challenged. And because the traditional African American self is still not yet fully accepted in corporate or professional America, the typical African American professional must conform to a Euro-centric definition of appropriate attire and speech, regardless of her competency or productivity levels. Some go so far as to report a sense of having to develop a second personality—one that satisfies corporate America, and one that helps them to survive in their own communities.

This, in itself, produces significant stress. Add to this, however, another, even more disparaging factor that most women of color face when they become successful in their careers. For many African American women the work entailed in seizing success, often means stepping into territory that is vastly different than their (humble) beginnings. For many, especially because of economics and other factors, reaching the goal has meant a level of dedication, commitment, and discipline that brought about significant changes in how they conduct their everyday lives. The graduate student who works full time and has a household to manage is usually not as available for social functions as she was prior to enrolling in graduate school. Although the notion of a family member pursuing professional advancement is usually touted as a wonderful thing, in many families there is a gross lack of understanding regarding the commitment required to achieve the goal. While family members verbalize support for advancement, many have only a limited, if any at all, understanding of the magnitude of the work entailed in the process. Families tend to feel alienated or in some cases, insulted when the aspiring professional member simply isn't as available for social functions as she was prior to her journey toward greatness. By the time she has reached her goals, there is mounting resentment within the family. Her loyalty to the family, to the community, and to Blackness, itself, may be questioned.

Among the most discouraging situations I've observed in clinical practice are the faces of women who have braved the gales of academic and professional achievement only to find that their families are not as enthusiastic about their accomplishments. The unfortunate fact is that not all Black women are supported through their efforts to achieve, either academically or professionally. Black women in professional and educational settings have described situations of being the butt of family jokes because of their extended educational pursuits. They are tauntingly referred by family members as the "professional student", or asked questions like "…you're *still* in school?" Still others are accused of being less than Black for wanting to pursue higher goals. Some African American women high achievers have had to deal with envy by siblings and/or other relatives as a result of their success. As if the insults listed above weren't already enough, some of these women report yet another assault to their professional development efforts. Many high earning African American women disclose their families' expectations that they (the newly professional) become a source of ready loans, gifts and other resources for family members who are doing little or nothing to advance their own status in life. When these women opt out of financially supporting relatives they are usually accused of having forgotten from whence they came. Typically the newly arrived Black female may fall prey to these kinds of family ploys, with guilt being the catalyst for doling out unwarranted cash to able bodied family members. Generally, however, these women wise up pretty quickly and get beyond this type of abuse.

Clinically, the SBW struggles more, it seems, when her intimate partner pulls the rug out from under her than when extended family alienates her. What may be the ultimate betrayal for most women pursuing greater heights educationally and/or professionally is when their partners renege on their support. Women share situations of having discussed in great detail with partners what their plans were and that partners agreed to support and stand by them through the process. Even in instances where intimate partners are not expected to finance their growth, it seems important for these women that their partners are there for them and with them. A few women questioned the value of their success when there was no one with whom to share it. There seems to be at least two commonly reported reasons for spouses to back out with their support for their professionally aspiring SBW. Some partners get cold feet after outside forces suggest that the person pursuing her dream will leave him once she's achieved her goals. This is not at all an uncommon complaint of men whose partners are pursuing academic and professional advancement. The primary source of such notions typically seem to be friends and family members who themselves have a limited understanding of the efforts entailed in professional advancement. These "friends" point out to an already insecure spouse the differences in his wife's social behaviors, especially with regard to her availability for social and family functions. Others taunt him with myths about her not needing him anymore and that he will somehow become subservient to her, or more notably, to her social status, salary or salary potential. The taunting often escalates to heated debates, with the SBW's partner becoming increasingly desperate and fearful of losing face in his community. While this notion seems wholly without merit, it has become a potent factor in African American marriages where the female partner out-earns or out-classes her spouse. To assume that one's committed partner will leave the relationship solely because of her achievement speaks more to the issue of the brokenness of the relationship than to the achievement of the partner. Such relationships are already deeply fractured and dissolution is probably looming regardless of either partner's growth. This issue will be dealt with in greater detail later.

Other partners feel a challenge to their manhood when female partners start to out-earn them. This is a fairly common issue within relationships involving African American men, it seems. While men, as a whole, have been taught that it is their role to be breadwinners, most have adapted to a nontraditional family structure.

Lots of men have come to terms with the fact that their wives or female significant others are, or will become, the primary source of the household income. It is not uncommon that the male in this family constellation comes to appreciate his wife's earnings. He rejoices in the fact that her earnings not only relieves him of the sole or primary economic burden for the household, but that it also allows the family greater opportunities for leisure as well as for luxury items. For African American families, this male-female wage differential continues to be much more of an issue. Although this is not usually the presenting issue in the clinical setting, generally it turns out to be the underlying problem, even (and probably especially) in cases of infidelity. The true issue isn't necessarily one of money, for money's sake, but rather, the meaning that money carries for the male. Usually money translates into power. In essence, then, whomever brings home the most money, in most people's minds at least, has the distinction within the family constellation as being the most powerful. For the African American male, who might perceive himself as having little power elsewhere in his life, salary poses a significant question to his identity. Further, African American men have traditionally been taught that their households are the one thing over which they have true dominion. These men have been taught that their home is the only place that they own and can control fully—free from the voice of the white man; free from systemic control and interference; free from any outside force. The paradox of this issue for

African American families is resounding and profound. As discussed earlier in this chapter, African American women are currently attaining educational levels that far exceed those of African American men. Consequently, African American women are earning significantly more than their peers. Therefore in a Black male/Black female intimate relationship it is more common than not that the female will indeed earn more than her male partner. Because it is nearly inevitable that the female will out-earn the male in Black male/Black female relationships, I strongly encourage males to reconsider their conceptualization of intimate partnerships.

Most of us grew up in homes where the father was the primary wage earner, and as such had the distinction of being the "king of the castle". Whether his highness' reign was real or imagined, his public persona was of one upon whom his family relied almost solely, or at least primarily. The men of this era were assured of one thing, if nothing else—their families needed them. Literally. They were assured that their families could not survive without their financial support. With the queen now earning as much, and in a lot of cases, considerably more than the king, his majesty is best served by re-thinking his notion of his role in the family. He must consider his contributions to the family constellation in ways other than merely financial. He must consider qualities he brings to the table other than that of a breadwinner. The questions asked to men in counseling sessions that seem to provoke some thought on this issue are: "Do you honestly think that all you mean to your wife is a paycheck?" "Do you think she would/should have married just anybody who earns what you earn?"

Rather than lessening the need for emotional support, these conditions faced by the SBW can tax her to the point of becoming emotionally paralyzed. Without question, the need for a secure and supportive outlet to vent challenges and to relax one's guard increases dramatically under such circumstances. When the heat is on at work as well as from extended family and friends, it is incumbent upon partners to demonstrate support, encouragement, and emotional safety for someone who may, at times, and for her own protection, appear to be tough and stoic.

-4-
"…she can do it all, and all by herself;
she doesn't need me".

EVEN SUPERWOMAN NEEDS TO CRY SOMETIMES

This seems to be one of the most dangerous myths regarding the SBW—it is dangerous to her psyche; it is dangerous to the psyche of her intimate partner; it is dangerous to their relationship; it is dangerous to the African American community, as it perpetuates a notion that is ridiculous, impossible, and will adversely affect the development of healthy relationships within African American communities for generations to come. As damning and as blatantly unrealistic as this notion is, it's one that seems to come up time and time again in the counseling arena. When the SBW and her partner are attempting to mediate interpersonal and interrelationship issues, the notion of her seemingly untiring resilience and strength turns up as an underlying issue almost routinely. Intimate partners of SBW sometime become so intimidated by their mates that they lose sight of them as women and as partners in relation to them. They also lose sight of their own value and role in their relationships.

Unfortunately when his ego becomes bruised with the notion that he is not needed, he will seek out situations were he believes he is needed. He will very probably comfort his ego via infidelity. This fact is borne out both empirically and anecdotally. When men perceive that they've been outclassed or dethroned by their wives' accomplishments they seek out extra-marital or otherwise socially unsanctioned affairs. What's interesting, however, (and it makes perfect sense when you consider the dynamics at work), is that the women with whom these men have affairs are generally women over which the men feel they have some significant dominion or control. Unfaithful men, themselves, describe the women in their illegitimate relationships as people over which they feel socially, and financially, superior; women they thought they were 'better' than, or whom they saw as being "beneath" them and certainly of lower social and intellectual status than their wives. This, again, makes perfect sense. Because the male in a relationship with a strong Black female may see his power in the relationship dissipating, he will tend to seek out relationships where he, indeed, has power. He then, would hardly choose someone of the similar intellectual, social or professional status as his legitimate partner. The social and educational caliber of unmarried women in extramarital affairs with married men is routinely less than that of the women in legitimate relationships with these men. These women's lower social and professional status provides the men with a significant ego boost, albeit artificial and temporary. The wives or legitimate partners of men who have had socially unsanctioned relationships are generally insulted by the betrayal itself, but are usually appalled by the caliber of women with whom their husbands have consorted.

Understanding this mechanism commonly used by men to soothe their egos, as stated earlier in this section, should not be taken as condoning this behavior. It is not the position of this book or this author to suggest that such behavior is anything less than socially, emotionally, and morally destructive. The wounded male ego is what is in question and is what needs repairing. History tells us that betrayal of trust does not mend egos or anything else, for that matter. It becomes the responsibility of the whole (mature) man to recognize his own frailties and to go about the business of fixing what is broken. It is also his responsibility to resist the urge to react to his own insecurities, lest he reek havoc on many lives, his own included. It is incumbent upon him to own his problems and to seek long term solutions, if indeed the relationship is of any value to him. For some men it is easier to hop from relationship to relationship than to deal with the real issue—himself.

The fact of the matter is this—and it is quite simple, really. None of us lives in a vacuum. We are dynamic and ever changing creatures and our very existence is contingent upon the existence and behaviors of other people. We can usually grasp this idea in terms of our physiological interdependence, but we seem to struggle a bit when owning our emotional interdependence. That's probably because the consequences or rewards of our emotional interdependence is not so concrete—if our emotional needs are not met our heart won't stop beating; it just may grow hardened; if our emotional needs go constantly ignored our bodies won't necessarily die, but our spirits will. On an emotional level, I submit to you that our need to connect, to belong, to interact is probably far more demanding than our physiological needs, at least in terms of the effort we must exert to be satisfied in this domain.

Keeping our emotional health intact requires great effort, carries great risk, but pays off in more profound rewards. No one, regardless of how much they know, how much money they earn, or how much property they own, is without need of other people.

It seems so unreasonable to me as a practitioner as well as a human being to assume that achievement of long sought and hard won goals would necessarily render a person less than needing of her basic emotional needs and supports. The frequency with which this underlying issue comes to the practice session gives indication of its potency as a factor in the destruction of Black male and female relationships. Certainly, the Black professional woman has amassed a great deal of training and expertise in her chosen field, with the by-product being a higher level of confidence and finesse that will be evident in most domains of her life. Her skillfulness in her field does not mean, however, that she has ceased being a woman; it does not mean that she does not have the emotional and psychological needs of a woman; it does not mean that she no longer needs to lean on the shoulder of the man she loves; it does not mean that she does not have insecurities and doubts about herself that she continues to work on interpersonally. What I've discovered is that she'd like that safe place where she can shed the corporate suit and the persona that goes with it and just be your lady—completely vulnerable; completely accepted; and completely safe.

-5-
"So, How Do I Partner with the SBW?"

EVEN SUPERWOMAN NEEDS TO CRY SOMETIMES

Although there are a few qualities that almost immediately come to mind when this question arises, I must tell you that there is no mystery, magic, or secret formula that will make your partnership with a strong black woman necessarily successful. Rather, its more an issue of common sense and security—your level of security in who you are and the value you bring to the relationship. While in a few minutes we will discuss five very basic principles to which you should subscribe when considering an intimate relationship with anyone, for now lets consider a few don'ts with regard to such partnerships. First, you should not enter these, or any relationship, for that matter, expecting, wanting, or otherwise desiring that the relationship will elevate you socially, professionally, or in some other way. Wherever you are, or aren't in your life is solely your responsibility. Your relationship with another human being should not be the mechanism you use to necessarily bring yourself to a position of power, status, or visibility. Secondly, I encourage you to not approach the relationship as a conquest. It is often said of men that they like the chase; they like to conquer. When the conquest is over what happens to the kill? (And yes, you do know there will be kill). If considering a relationship is for the sole purpose of the gratification of your ego, let me be the first to tell you that you are not in a good place emotionally. My suggestion is that you run (not walk) to your nearest mental health professional. While I can think of a lot more prohibitions regarding partnering with a strong Black woman, I think it is time better spent to focus now on the five principles that, if internalized and applied in your life, will guide you to an emotionally and otherwise productive relationship. We cannot begin a discussion of the five relationship principles that facilitate emotionally adaptive relationships without talking, at least briefly, about intimacy.

We tend to subscribe to a pretty narrow definition of intimacy. More often than not the word brings to mind images of physical contact. Although this is not necessarily inaccurate, this definition begs to be broadened. While intimacy does indeed imply proximity, closeness, or even touching, to leave it at the superficial domain of the physical does not do the concept justice, and leaves us with a shallow conceptualization of a term that connotes profound levels of bonding. I am advised and often advise mentees, students, and clients that when aiming for real intimacy in a relationship, sex should not be a necessary objective. I'm not suggesting that sex is not an important component of a viable long term relationship, but that in many cases it serves as a distraction to other relational activities that promote intimacy. Sex is exactly that—sex. It implies nothing more than physical joining of two bodies. It is not a bad thing, but it is not the foundation for intimacy. Any attempt to build a viable relationship on sex alone will be futile. Such a relationship is no more than a ticking bomb—just waiting to blow up in your face. Actually your energies would be better spent on some far flung project like digging your way to China. Conversely, the bond founded on a combination of love, respect, trust, and knowledge between partners stands a far greater chance of being fulfilling. A relationship built on love, respect, and trust is one that can withstand the acknowledgment of flaws both within and outside the relationship, and can devise and implement measures to protect the relationship from injury. This level of knowing onself and being with oneself both within and outside of the relationship assures one of togetherness, yet separateness. Bonding on this level is not fearful of change, but rather embraces change and moves with it. Intimacy that surpasses the physical relationship is rooted first and foremost in self assuredness. Not egoism. Not narcissism. Intimacy within a relationship starts with a sense of comfort with who and what you are as an individual, and what you stand for as a person as well as as a partner. Then, and only then, can we accept and develop comfort with others, even when they are flagrantly different.

1) GET TO KNOW HER

Every woman is an individual with a unique set of traits and a proportional relationship among traits that sets her totally apart from any other person on this planet. It doesn't matter that she's earned the same degrees as her friend or that she has the same type of job as your sister, or that she likes to read, just like the lady who sits next to her in the church choir. We can become so hurried about making a relationship into something palatial that we forget to get to know the person with whom we're partnering. What is her favorite color? What is her daddy's middle name? Has she ever been a bridesmaid in a wedding? What did her prom dress look like? What is her blood type? What is her philosophy about life? What is her stance on same-gender education? I am saddened by marital couplings that have been in existence for more than five years where the husband really doesn't know his wife. I take it as an indication of his lack of interest in her, and therefore in her needs. More often than not, the wife is intimately knowledgeable about her husband, and over the years, has invested the time and effort to get to know him. Getting to know your female partner is not rocket science, and it certainly does not entail any clandestine activity. It's a mere matter of being interested in her... interested enough to want to know who she is and what she's about; interested enough, simply, to ask.

Engaging in deep conversation seems to be the most rational route to get what you need from her. It is important that there be conversations. Note the "s" at the end of the word 'conversation'—meaning more than one conversation. Yes, this means actually talking; lots of talking. We live in a fast paced world. We want things quick. We want them in a hurry. Whatever we're asking for, we realized we would like to have had it yesterday. We thrive in instant gratification. We are accustomed to pushing a button and getting it quick, fast, and in a hurry—- we want our meals prepared and served in the snap of a finger; we want our photographs before they come out of the camera; For some of you these next few sentences will be nothing short of heartbreaking, but you must know that there are some things, I'm happy to report, that still have to be done the old fashioned way. In the case of learning about another person on an emotionally intimate level, it simply is not going to be instantaneous. Developing the emotional intimacy needed to create viability in the relationship is a deliberate process that requires an investment of time, energy, and patience. This seems even more important when considering an intimate partnership with the SBW, as she is a goal-oriented person who thrives on accomplishing tasks. You must be absolutely sure that you understand her, her goals, what drives her, her expectations of you, what she brings to the relationship and what she hopes to gain from the relationship. She will be expecting you to be a part of the goal setting team, and further, to play an active role in realizing the relational goals.

2) DEVELOP AN APPRECIATION FOR WHO SHE IS,

One of the biggest mistakes we make in relationships is seeing a person, not for who or what she is, but for what you believe is her potential "to be". More often than not we consider a few outward qualities, and somewhere in the recesses of our minds we start the process of forming her into that ideal person. You know—- that person who is just perfect for you. Each one of us is so incredibly imperfect ourselves, that it is difficult to imagine what we would do with a perfect person. In fact most of us have adapted so well to our own imperfections that we are truly oblivious to them. Even a person who complements all of our own imperfections would be a challenge to our tolerance.

Nonetheless, we spend inordinate amounts of time and energy pasting together in our minds the notion of the perfect mate. In our minds eyes we see the perfect body size and contour; we envision perfect eyes, hair, and skin color; we imagine educational levels; income levels, and on and on. When we meet a person who has a few of the qualities we desire, we tend to hurriedly scoop them up with every intention of filling in the blanks ourselves. We adopt the view that whatever he or she is missing, I can "help" him or her become. Actually, women, more often than men seem to be pretty notorious for this line of reasoning. Way too frequently we go into relationships with all intent on remaking the poor unsuspecting suitor. While this phenomenon appears to be more common with women, it is not altogether absent from the repertoire of plans men have for their brides-to-be.

My suggestion to either gender: Do him/her a favor; do yourself a favor, and do the universe a favor—if you cannot accept the individual for who he or she is, it is only prudent to leave her alone. Don't try to remake her to fit a mold that you've developed in your own head. The vision you have of the ideal woman is not real—it is merely a figment of fantasy, designed by you to appease your short term interest. In the relationship, and because of the relationship, along with other factors in your lives, you both will grow and evolve . A year down the road, for example, neither of you will be exactly the same person you were the day you met. She brings assets and liabilities to the relationship just as you do. Those traits that she brings are uniquely hers. The combination of your unique traits and her unique traits is what makes your relationship uniquely yours. There will never be another relationship like the one you will have with her. There will never be another relationship like the one you had with your old girlfriend or ex-partner. It is important not to make her be someone from your past. Each time you see her, think of her, hear her voice, smell her perfume, you should make an effort to get comfortable with the knowledge that she is one-of-a-kind. There is not another person in existence exactly like her. You must also grow comfortable with the notion that she is who she is and not an art project that you need to re-mold. Simply put, she is who she is. Either you can accept that fully, or you can't. If you can't then your only option is to move on.

The process of developing an appreciation for your SBW is much like the process of getting to know her—it will take time and effort; lots of time and lots of effort. It will mean an investment of your energies to accept those things about her that may be inconsistent with your current belief system regarding women, women's roles, women's behaviors, and maybe even something as basic as women's attire.

3) SUPPORT HER AND HER INTERESTS

Once you're comfortable with who she is and those unique traits of hers, then you'll know that she's pretty adamant about her success. You'll know she's a pretty disciplined person. You will have learned by now that she is goal-directed and focused on her growth as well as the growth and well being of the relationship. You will have known by now that she is a doer; a risk taker, of sorts; that she is not a procrastinator. You'll know that she's thirsty for movement—interpersonally, emotionally, financially, professionally, and so on.

You've done your homework, so you know that trying to hold her back is not an option. She aspires to greatness and she'd like you to take the journey with her. You have a choice—support her or walk away now. Supporting her may or may not mean writing a check every quarter. I suspect most cases of supporting your SBW translates into being there for her; being her cheerleader; encouraging her when the 'night has been too lonely and road has been too long'. Supporting her may mean listening to her tell you about the horrible day she had at the office, or basking with her in glory when she has achieved some great feat at work or at school. Support may mean defending her honor when family is coming down hard on her because she missed yet another family festivity. It may mean covering for her at Sunday school when work assignments and school assignments are off-the-chart overwhelming. Supporting your SBW may mean all of these things; and it may mean not a single one. Support will mean different things for different couples, but what it will mean is that you've got her back—ALL THE TIME! After all, isn't that what partners do?

As human beings we are dynamic—constantly evolving. To try to stop that process is like trying to stop Tuesday from happening at 11:58 PM on Monday night. Pretty futile. Most of us fail to encourage our partners' growth because we fear movement ourselves. We get so comfortable with the way things were when we first met that we want to freeze those moments in time. My suggestion is simply to purchase a camera. Other than your own personal recollection of an event, a photograph is probably the best you can do to preserve any moment. Whether you like it or not, change will occur. Change IS a condition of life! So, try as you might, Tuesday is coming. The fear of change can be paralyzing to an individual, and more so to a relationship. Since we can all relate to money, I will use a financial analogy here. It is sometimes helpful to think of our relationships as investments. Our goal in investing is to yield growth—to have more money at the end of the investment period than we had starting out. We don't just WANT our investments to grow; we actually EXPECT them to grow. For that to happen we seek the best financial advice we can get and assume the risks inherent in the growth process. Although we try to minimize our risks, the fact of risk is a given, and we assume the risk in hopes of a fruitful yield. We do our homework and try to choose stocks that have good growth potential. If we thought a particular stock was going to retain the same value across the life of the investment period, I'm doubtful that most of would consider it a wise place to invest our monies. After all, we want growth! We want movement!.

We want the same (if we're emotionally healthy) for and from our interpersonal relationships. We want to be more in love; we want to trust more; we want to have greater respect for our mates. In order to get these kinds of returns, we've got to encourage and support growth, in partners, as well as in ourselves. As her partner, you have an obligation to support and encourage her growth. As someone who loves, respects, and honors her, it seems you would want to see your bud blossom into the beautiful rose she aspires to be.

4) APPROACH THE RELATIONSHIP AS A PARTNERSHIP; NOT AS A COMPETITION

The word "partnership" conjures up images of alliance or association between two or more people for work toward a common goal. This alliance is formed because one partner alone cannot reach the goal, and because the two bring complementary assets, that together, will facilitate the process of goal attainment. Partners pursuing a common interest must respect one another's assets, and must trust each other to put forth the effort required to reach the goal. This is generally true in almost any type of partnering relationship—business, educational, social, personal, or interpersonal. Making the decision to enter a committed relationship, whether this be marriage or monogamous dating, is a pretty serious venture. It is one that should be approached with care, with prudence, and with knowledge. In addition to getting to know the woman to whom you're considering committing, it is imperative that you actually know yourself. Entry into the relationship is not a decision to be taken lightly, as it means exclusivity by both of you. It means that you and your mate have opted to invest your time, your energies, and your emotions in a relationship that is uniquely yours; it means neither of you are looking at other intimate relationship options, but rather are focused on making the best of the one you've created. It means you have planted a seed that you fully hope and expect to come to maturity. It means that you understand that to bring your seed to maturity that you give yourself to nurturing it wholeheartedly. Like any good partnership, your relationship, too, will have goals that you will set together. Each of you will bring different strengths to the relationship that will facilitate you reaching your goals. Your strengths should complement one another. For those areas where either or both of you are deficient, you will strategize for the most effective and efficient means of reaching your goals. I liken the spousal/partnering relationship to that of maneuvering a john boat on a lake or pond. In the john boat each of you has an oar, and together, are expected to steer the boat to the other side of the lake. As long as you both are rowing at about equal pace, the boat will continue to move straight ahead. Should one of you stop rowing the boat while the other continues, however, the boat will only go around in circles. Do you see the futility in this situation? In order to set the boat back on course and move towards your goal, the single rowing partner must row twice as hard. This works for a while, but the extra demands on the one rowing partner will eventually wear him or her out. When the only rowing person is too worn out to keep going, the boat will drift, directionless. This, unfortunately, happens in relationships. One partner who really isn't committed to the work in a relationship gets tired or distracted and quits. The other partner works twice as hard to keep the relationship on course, but can only sustain this pace for so long. Eventually the relationship goes adrift.

Both women and men considering intimate partnerships are as guilty as the other of assuming that their goals are consistent with the other's. It is imperative that partners have common goals. If you're not working toward a common goal, you really have no partnership. If you share a common household but not common relational goals, you're nothing more than roommates. Couples frequently commit to relationships with no discussion of their goals. It is not surprising that 36 months into the relationship things simply fall apart. It helps the process to actually talk about goals and to set objectives to assess movement.

Too often, men see the strong black woman as something to be conquered. Entering a partnership with anything other than the intent to be full partners is irresponsible, selfish, and emotionally maladaptive. Competition is okay for the basketball court or the race track, but certainly not for people's lives. The people in a partnership are actually allies—they are on the same side;

working for a common goal. They are supposed to work together, not against one another. A partnership is not about trying to one-up each other, but rather more about strategizing together to find effective ways to achieve whatever your goals are. Despite how smart she is or how much money she earns, the SBW really needs you and the skills and traits you bring to the relationship. As tough as you think she is, she simply cannot row the boat all by herself. I encourage prospective partners to be certain they are actually up to the task of rowing the boat for the long term.

The novice will read this and think it is all too complicated; too mechanical. He will profess vehemently and in the spirit of the true romantic, that all two people need to make it work is love. As heartwarming as this notion sounds, it simply isn't true. While love certainly is a vital component of the adaptive spousal relationship, it, by itself, has little to do with sustaining workable relationships. In addition to love, formulating a true partnership requires trust, respect, honesty, and loyalty. Please note that these are not optional—they simply **must** be present. Lets talk about trust first, since we seem to ration or set contingencies on the distribution of our trust. We treat trust as if it were a terminal trait that we will run out of. We say things like ' I don't trust her because she…' The fact of the matter is that it doesn't really matter what she does, has done or will do. In other words, our ability to trust and certainly our choice to trust is exactly that—a choice. And one that we make freely, and willingly, I might add. We choose to trust another human being. Another person's actions or history may factor into the decision to trust, but make no mistake, <u>another person's actions or history does not prohibit anyone from the ability to trust.</u> More often than not, the prohibition to trust comes from our knowledge of ourselves. We tend to judge others, especially in matters of the heart, by what we know we are capable of, or by what we know we have a history of doing. In essence then, we often do not trust our mates because we do not trust ourselves. We don't believe ourselves to be worthy of another's trust, and can't, then, see another as being worthy of our trust. We also cite unpleasant relational experiences as reasons not to trust. This again, is more about us than about the next person. Of course, discretion and prudence should be exercised as we enter any new relationship, however, we must remember too, that each relationship is a completely separate entity and should be evaluated on its own merits. Some would argue, and I concur, that the rewards of loving and having been loved far outweigh the pain of a broken heart.

Assuming you've opted to enter into a partnership with a SBW, you must be willing to turn the page and start the process of writing this new chapter. Writing the new chapter does not entail a denial of your past. It means that we take those lessons from our past and apply them to the formulation of a healthy partnership. In doing so, then, you will make a decision to trust her, and to do so fully. No, there is no guarantee that things won't go south, but aren't the prospects of a fulfilling relationship worth the risk?

DR. D. HANN MORRISON, PH. D, LPC

African American women treading the waters of academic and professional achievement must deal with the challenges of racism and sexism on an almost routine basis—her competency is questioned because of the color of her skin; she is put under the microscope constantly; if she doesn't assert herself boldly, she is considered not to be management material; when she does assert herself, she's labeled aggressive; and should she express a dissenting opinion, she's marked an 'angry black female'. It is no wonder she has developed into a no-nonsense, pragmatic, no-time-to-play-games person. She expects directness in her professional life as well as in her personal life. She expects loyalty from the one person who professes to love and respect her. She expects the shoulder he offered to actually be there for her. For the strong black woman, her achievements are not just hers, but rather are her's and her partner's together—she expects him to share in the glory as well as to slosh with her through the muddy waters of disappointment, hurt, and betrayal. She expects him to be her cheerleader and to defend her honor and her efforts in the face of any and all detractors.

The strong black women, based on who she is, how she operates in her personal and professional life, commands respect. Her commitment to her goals and her demonstration of discipline in achieving them, usually commands great respect. She is a woman of which many are in awe—wonderment, even. It is not unusual that her intimate partner, too, is in awe of her. More often than I care to recall, he comes to question whether he deserves to be with a woman of her social, intellectual, or professional stature. This is a valid indication that his respect for her has turned into intimidation. With this unyielding focus on her achievements, he has lost sight of her as a woman, as a person, as a partner in the relationship with him. The question the SBW's partner is really asking isn't about her or her achievements, but rather about himself. He is calling into question how secure he is in his own right, not just as a partner in the relationship. These nagging questions should serve as his alarm clock. Time to wake up and do something constructive about himself.

###

Honesty seems an almost natural part of a relationship that is rooted in respect, love, and loyalty, however, since deceit is the weapon that breaches the relational foundation, I thought it prudent to offer at least a short discourse on the issue. Lying to one's partner may actually be a good indication of the lack of these other traits in the relationship—it indicates that you do not trust her, with the facts, at least; it indicates that you do not have enough respect for her to believe that she can manage facts; and it puts into question whether or not you believe that she is actually deserving of the truth. In the presence of these sentiments, I would suggest that the relationship is already compromised. A relationship built on half-truths, misinformation, or flagrant misrepresentation of fact is, simply put, not a relationship. It is no more than someone's fantasy, and a desperate one, at that. It is not how things are, but rather a representation of how you'd like things to be; it is not the way it is, but rather the way you wish it were. Because lying in your interpersonal relationship takes so much more work than telling the truth, the games become difficult to sustain. Because one lie requires another for justification, we often become confused with what we've told whom, and when and why, and…. Yes, it becomes exhausting, and when you've painted yourself in a corner, as you surely will do, your little house of cards is bound to crumble. And when it does, trying to sort out fact from fiction is often too monumental a task for the people who've been insulted and emotionally assaulted by your games.

Everything we've experienced—every action, every thought, every idea, every single behavior—be they good, bad, or indifferent, goes into making us who we are today.

We have to own all those parts of ourselves, and believe that the person in partnership with us is also accepting of all those parts. If she is not fully accepting of you, then forming a partnership is not an option. Your partnership is significantly breached when you feel the need to tell lies, either about former or current behaviors.

For some people, men, it seems, more so than women, deceit has become an ingrained part of what they believe constitutes male-female interactions. The truth has become alien to their tongues. Years of conditioning from fathers, older brothers, or extended family members have taught some men that lying in the intimate relationship is a way of life. They learn as early as in their teen years to simply not tell their girlfriends the truth, and they're rewarded for this type of behavior by acceptance into the boys' club. They continue this practice into adulthood with wives and babies' mammas. Some men have become so accustomed to lying, that the notion of honesty in their interpersonal relationships just doesn't enter their scope of thought. These people may voice a desire for intimacy, but they are merely playing a destructive game with themselves and their partners. These men are out to conquer the women they pursue. This type of relationship should not, by any means, be confused with a partnership. It is merely a personal quest. Saddest of all, in these cases, the subduer, himself, isn't sure of what it is he is out to conquer. He just knows he has to out-do his mate, and in his immature way, resorts to primitive measures. These men are looking to "one-up" their mates in some pathological pursuit of power. The question has been asked whether a SBW can respect a strong Black male who does not conquer or overwhelm everything in the path of his goal. My response is a resounding and unequivocal "YES". Absolutely! Yes, the SBW can and does respect her less-than-super-human male partner. From the perspective of a true intimate partnering, she doesn't expect him to run through life like an out-of-control tornado, taking down everything in his path. She expects him to be a profoundly human (human) being—complete with assets as well as liabilities. She expects to depend on him, and expects that he will also depend on her. She respects that he can own and articulate that he isn't the master of all things

When I come across men who operate under the illusion that they must conquer all, including their intimate partners, I encourage them to look deeply within themselves and consider these questions: What is it you are afraid of? Who is it that you really don't trust? What does happiness look like to you?

For people with problems of honesty in their interpersonal relationships, the issue is usually one of honesty with themselves. The self esteem of chronic liars is pretty low, and they question if they, themselves, are worthy or deserving of truth. Through their misrepresentations they are trying to re-invent themselves and their worlds. These people are notorious for a tendency towards a series of short term, passion-filled relationships that are easily entered into, and just as easily walked away from. They step in and out of relationships with great ease because their investments are minimal and therefore their relationships have little depth. In the therapeutic arena, they typically present as vague and shallow, and with only a limited knowledge or understanding about themselves. They typically don't know themselves and dread investing the time and energy with themselves to get to know who they are. While I cannot imagine any sane adult who would see the benefit of this kind of relationship hopping, any of us can check out the Centers for Disease Control (CDC) (cdc.gov) website and see that this behavior has dangerous ramifications. The CDC data paints a very sobering picture. HIV/AIDS are ravaging the African American community. Aside from the AIDS issue, these people are desperately looking for something. That something, unbeknownst to them, cannot be found in another person. What they have yet to realize is that the process of filling the emptiness they're feeling can only start by looking deep within themselves. These people rarely achieve any level of quality within their relationships…they NEVER achieve true intimacy.

5) SPEND TIME WORKING ON YOURSELF

Although I've chosen to make this item the final of five guiding principles to facilitate true intimacy with the SBW, it does not mean it has any less value than the others. In fact, I would suspect that spending time working on yourself is something you would want to consider a priority. In fact, I will just go ahead, as a practicing counselor, and recommend that you make it number one on your list and, further, that you commit to self improvement whether or not you're intimately involved or considering an intimate involvement with a SBW. I feel the need to clarify here, that self improvement does not necessarily mean that you should run out and enroll in college tomorrow. This is the furthest thing from the truth. As much as I value education, I firmly believe it is something you should pursue because you want to, not because your partner has earned a certain degree. Secondly, while the sense of accomplishment that comes with earning a degree or other educational attainment may contribute to one's sense of well being, please understand, that a degree, in and of itself, will not make you whole. There are lots of men (and women, too) with a string of alphabets behind their names who are more broken than the high school drop out. When I speak of working on oneself, I'm talking about engaging in activities that will render you more secure and accepting of the person you are. It is only when you become comfortable with you that you can look at intimacy as a healthy adaptive adult function. It is only when you are secure and accepting of who you are that you will understand that you are a good person, worthy and deserving of love and respect. It is only when you come to the realization that you are worthy and deserving of love, that you will actually love you and, more importantly, you will actually like you. Not until you like and love yourself, can you love another human being. Remember, the chain is only as strong as

its weakest link. It doesn't necessarily matter how emotionally stable your mate is, the relationship is only as strong and viable as the least adaptive partner. It is incumbent upon each party in the relationship, then, to aspire to, and maintain optimal emotional health. Until all these things happen, your contribution to a healthy relationship is questionable, at best.

There are many ways we can engage in self improvement. Almost any mechanism that will better your physical body, your mind, and/or your emotional state can be part of your self improvement effort. Since we are constantly evolving, dynamic creatures, we can always grow. We can grow by taking on new assignments and/or responsibilities at work, in the community, or even at home—reading a book; learning the keyboard; assuming a leadership position with a local organization; joining a local organization whose mission is consistent with your interests and values. Many people look in the mirror on New Years Day and decide that an investment in self might mean shedding a few pounds. Others consider exercising, either joining a gym or going to the track solo. Improving oneself can cover such a vast array of activities, with really only one criteria—whatever the activity or undertaking, it should contribute to your personal, physical, emotional, mental, and/or spiritual good. If the activity contributes to your betterment it will undoubtedly contribute to the betterment of your interpersonal relationship.

Too often when people couple, they tend to forget about themselves as individuals. You and your SBW are a couple, yet each of you are still individuals—with unique interests and unique needs. It is important that you not lose sight of this fact. Having your own interest does not mean you are betraying your spouse. It simply means that there is a healthy respect between the two of you that allows for personal as well as relationship growth. It is also important that you have your own time to spend exclusively with you. Much like your spouse having her own time to pursue her individual interests.

WORKING ON SELF FROM THE INSIDE OUT

Working to improve oneself from the inside out is hard work. I would venture that this might be some of the hardest work you've ever done. I don't want you to take on this enterprise naively. I also don't want you to be intimidated by it, either. It is work that you can do. It will require that you roll up your sleeves and get down and dirty with yourself; it will require you to flex emotional muscles you didn't know you had. Again, self improvement from the inside is HARD work, but the rewards are priceless. Let us consider at least three components of self improvement from the inside out: introspection; ownership; and dealing with your fear.

INTROSPECTION

The most fundamental step to working on oneself is probably going to be the most difficult. This is the one that requires you to come face to face with you. A few pages earlier I talked about the men who hop from relationship to relationship without ever taking a break in between to do some self assessment. I declared that these men are generally afraid—that they dread being alone with themselves. What, you might ask, could be so dreadful about being alone? I believe there are actually two issues at the core of this fear. One is the fear of not belonging…of not being connected to another person. Some people have no definition separate and apart from a relationship. These people cannot see themselves outside a relationship. So desperate are they, that any relationship will do. To these people, who are truly emotionally needy, even a horribly broken relationship is better than no relationship. This phenomenon seems to be observed more frequently in women than in men, but is not altogether uncommon in men. Their need for companionship is so intense that these people do not see themselves as viable entities when or if they're not in a relationship. The second issue operating in these situations actually fertilizes the first. These people really don't know themselves. Having no real sense of identity places one in the position of allowing another person, or a relationship to assign an identity. So, the great challenge inherent in being alone is getting to know that person in the mirror—facing some cold hard truths about themselves. The most challenging part of the task of working on yourself will be to take that look in the mirror; to look introspectively at who you really are. If you've been living an illusion for 40 or 50 years, it will be chilling to deal with the truth. This is not to say that what you'll discover will be negative, but it might certainly be different. The truth may very well be refreshing, but it will be different. It will mean that you will have to adapt––you will have to change, and this, to many people, is also a great source of anxiety. As you read this book I suspect you saw yourself in portions of it. That image might not have been so flattering, and so, the tendency was to ignore it, or worse, to deny it. The good news is that you've made it to this section. You hadn't just tossed this book aside, or if you did, you've picked it back up. That says that you, for whatever reason, are ready to at least initiate the process of evolving into the adaptive adult partner your SBW wants, expects, and deserves. It say's that maybe you're tired of pseudo-intimacy, and at this age or stage in your life you want a relationship that is built on a solid foundation. You have looked inside and opted to consider that the misery in your own life is not the fault of an overbearing mother or an abusive father, or a nagging ex-wife. You've decided to take a look into that mirror to see if the person there might have some clue to what is not right in your life. What brought you to this point in the book is of little consequence—-the point is you are here. You are at least considering the journey to a higher level of emotional responsibility.

Our best introspective work is done when we are not actually in a romantic relationship. This is defined as quality time alone taking inventory of yourself. Not being burdened with the responsibilities inherent in maintaining a relationship frees up our mental and emotional energies to focus on ourselves. It allows us to close old doors and to take care of our emotions (lick our wounds, so to speak) before taking the plunge into the next relationship. Actually, if you learn to space your relationships and take care of yourself between them, you'll find that you don't actually "plunge" into relationships, but rather you learn to step gracefully into new relationships without feeling desperate. Part of your introspective journey is to take inventory of your past relationships—take each one individually and review them carefully. How do your relationships generally start? Do they tend to start passionately or impulsively? Are you generally sexually active with women within a few weeks of meeting? Do your relationships typically start with you being on the prowl? Do you find yourself plunging right into the relationship? If you're answering yes to most of these questions, this might be a clue about your own level of emotional neediness, and what relationships represent for you. How do your relationships typically end? Is there a lot of drama associated with your endings? These aren't easy questions, but they are questions that demand honesty if you are ever to emerge from a place of potential self destruction. The only way to get to the true answers to these questions is to not be distracted by the superficial. You will require time alone. Without this "down time" you will undoubtedly carry old stuff into new relationships and repeat the drama cycle over and over again. Introspection requires that we learn to be alone without necessarily being lonely. The two words are not synonymous.

OWNERSHIP

The next step in growing is being willing to own those parts of ourselves that make us uncomfortable. It is only after we acknowledge that we have a problem can we engage in the process of fixing what is broken. So, as you see yourself in this book, dare to own what you see, and dare to acknowledge that your behaviors may have brought distress to the lives of people who trusted you with their emotions. Acknowledgment means assuming responsibility for your behaviors—not assigning blame to someone or something else. Remember, for every counterproductive behavior you've engaged in, you must own that you made a conscious decision to do so. You simply must own that. Its easy to blame someone else for your behaviors or to say you didn't mean to do a particular something—you didn't mean to lie to your wife; you didn't mean to cheat. Without knowing you personally, let me tell you something with great assuredness: whatever you do or have done; whatever behaviors you engage in;—- you fully intend to engage in. You may not have intended the outcome(s) to have been as they were, but yes, you meant to do all those things. Your behaviors are completely yours. You have free will and you make choices. I suspect in most cases, at least, that you just didn't mean to get caught.

Not meaning to get caught should not be confused with not meaning to engage in a particular behavior. Now that that's cleared up, lets get back to the crux of the discussion. A vital component of the ownership process involves understanding and accepting the impact your behaviors have had in and on the lives of the people you've injured (just like a punch to the lip is a physical assault, a betrayal is an emotional assault—both result in injury; its just that one of those injuries will heal much quicker than the other). You must also come to terms with the adverse impact your maladaptive behaviors have had on your life as well—how it has impacted your credibility; your respectability with your peers, with your children, with your colleagues.

You must own and accept that your selfishness and immaturity has caused great pain, sometimes even emotional devastation, in many other lives. You must recognize that for some of your victims the recovery process is a long and tedious journey. You have impacted some lives in ways that will actually dictate the course of their lives for the rest of their lives. You must not, then, minimize the magnitude of their pain by assuming that uttering the phrase "I'm sorry" will make it all okay. "I'm sorry" is a grossly overused phrase that is often a thinly disguised excuse for irresponsible behaviors. An extreme example of this callousness may be seen in the case involving a man who had had an extra marital affair with a young woman. The affair became pretty public, as it took place in a small town where they both lived. At the first suggestion that his wife would reconcile with him, this man abruptly and without provocation or discussion ended the affair. The net result of the affair for the female was public humiliation, blatant betrayal and a lasting dent in her reputation. The male could not understand why his (ex) mistress would be mad at him. His response to me when asked to explain his reasoning was "I told her 'I'm sorry'. She just needs to move on." He could not see how callous he was in offering this simple, almost meaningless phrase to a young woman whose life he had just about ruined. Not only did he have little empathy for what the lady must be going through, personally, emotionally, and especially socially, he seemed to have such a minimal understanding of the long term impact his action would have on her. What I found most astounding in this situation was that this man seemed to genuinely believe that using that phrase ('I'm sorry') gave him the right to be completely reckless, as long as he remembered to offer the ceremonial "I'm sorry" at the conclusion of his deeds. While it would seem that this situation is a bit more predatory than the breaches you have committed in your intimate relationships, don't assume that the hurt you've inflicted is any less damaging. The unfortunate fact is that this case is not uncommon. Men who cheat on their wives issue the same token apology and expect all to be well again in their households. They come in to therapy, not because he has betrayed her trust and damaged their marriage, but because he can't understand why his wife can't just get over it. Carrying around a pocket full of "I'm sorry's" to distribute to people as you injure them, either by design or by carelessness, is simply not acceptable. Instead, it smacks of blatant selfishness, immaturity, and borders on narcissism. The people you've injured do not need to hear "I'm sorry" from you. Your behaviors have already proven that you're sorry. What they need to know is that you accept full responsibility for your actions (without making ANY excuses), and that you are working to change your selfish ways. They need to believe that you are so genuine about the remorse for the injury you've caused that you are willing to invest the time and energy to work on yourself in the hopes you will not victimize others.

Toying with another person's emotions is grievous. Simply uttering the "phrase", as I call it, does not absolve you of responsibility. You have changed her life in ways you probably could not imagine, so you will understand then, that she does not want to be your friend. Once you've owned your actions and owned the impact they've had on you and others significant to you, then you can aspire to rise to a more emotionally adaptive level of functioning.

DEAL WITH YOUR FEARS

Owning your behaviors is a positive step in the direction toward wholeness, but, by itself isn't, enough to keep you from re-offending. You must seek out the root cause of your maladaptive behavior patterns. Assuming you are not significantly mentally ill, I would venture that fear lies at the root of most of the inappropriateness seen in your intimate relationships. When we are overwhelmed by fear and backed into a corner, we tend to strike at the most basic level and in the most primitive ways. I think it is important to talk about your fears. The ideal person with whom to have those conversations would be the person with whom you're trying to establish an emotionally enriching relationship. If this person is emotionally unavailable to hear you, this might be an omen of things to come. If you are uncomfortable sharing your innermost thoughts with your partner, then I would question how invested you are about developing intimacy in the relationship. If you're a bit apprehensive and fear overwhelming your partner, then the next best venue for this discussion would probably be a trained professional. Allow a counselor to facilitate the process between you and your partner. The important thing is that you give air to those issues that make you fearful. Trying to hide your fears behind machismo will get you back to a primitive way of responding to your mate. Remember, she didn't marry Clark Kent. She married you. She loves you. She respects you. She expects you to be her partner. Sharing your emotions with her is an honor that she will cherish, as it demonstrates to her that you trust and respect her and see value in her role in your life. And the broader the range of emotions you can show, gives her an idea of the depth of your trust.

Now that you know better, your next responsibility is to make a conscious decision to do better.

-6-

A final word to the Strong Black Woman

Just as I was about to close this book I had the great fortune of conversing with a colleague who's professional opinion I value greatly. In that conversation I discovered that there was a chapter missing from the book. Here is that chapter—actually it's not even a chapter, but rather a brief message, but a profound one, just the same. Chapter five provided principles and guidelines directed primarily towards males to facilitate the development and maintenance of healthy intimate relationships with SBW. Since relationships, by their very nature, require the full participation of at least two parties, I'd feel remiss if I didn't also use this forum to speak to SBW regarding what I see to be a pressing issue in the black male-female relationship. My colleague reminded me that when one is good at being strong, that same person may actually have difficulty being vulnerable, or at least articulating her vulnerability. As we gain competence in one area of our lives, it seems, we begin also to become more competent in other areas, as well. Ultimately, we become less than patient with incompetence or, more especially, with inefficiency. We work hard, managing demanding careers and even more demanding personal lives. We pull off what seems to be the impossible, and we do so with finesse, and a minimum (if any) whining. As we pull rabbits out of our hats all the time, we come to expect others in our lives to be able to do so as well. We have developed a low threshold for tolerance when we feel our mates aren't rowing the boat at break-neck speed. After all, we are pulling our relational load in addition to the other demands of our personal and professional lives. And, if the situation demanded, we wouldn't think twice about rowing for two. We lose faith when he doesn't seem to be trying as hard as we think he should be. And remember, the barometer by which we measure his actions is by our own efforts and accomplishments. Because people around us expect us to be strong, we somehow assume that we cannot be vulnerable. We have adopted the notion that we've got to weather every storm, and we've got to do it without a hint of fear or apprehension. We've learned that there is no place in our lives for a breach of any sort—we've got to keep the foundation intact at all times, lest we have failed.

I've learned, and want to convey here that being vulnerable is not without its challenges for almost anyone, as it exposes those parts of us, or issues about ourselves that leave us susceptible to hurt and disappointment. Being vulnerable means recognizing that we may not be as powerful or invincible as we would like to portray. It means that the SBW is incredibly human; incredibly less than perfect; incredibly flawed—needy, even. It means that the SBW's world may indeed fall apart sometimes; it means she cries; it means her heart aches; it means that she is sometimes scared to death. Articulating her vulnerability is probably the real struggle for the SBW. In conveying her needs, the SBW is tantamount to being stark naked in the presence of her partner; she is totally exposed. For many, this kind of exposure may or may not be responded to in a manner that is altogether sensitive or nurturing. Remember, people in our environment are accustomed to seeing us weather all kinds of storms. They've come to expect us to "handle our business". So being vulnerable, for the SBW is not just risky, but monumentally risky, as such may be the catalyst for disappointment by family, girlfriends, partners, or even society at large.

There is little doubt that these images of toughness that have been etched into the minds of women of color are far outside the realm of reality. It simply isn't reasonable to expect any human to be exposed to emotional extremes, then to mute his or her responses to these experiences. Couple these unrealistic expectations of stoicism with a series of unhealthy relationships and you end up with an angry resentful person who feels the strong need to protect herself through the very impassivity that we know to be counterproductive. When these circumstances exist, it is not only common, but actually realistic that these women would protect their emotional selves. The betrayed, the hurt, or the otherwise emotionally injured woman will tend to protect her feelings with guardedness. The tough, 'I don't need him' persona helps to form the protective brick wall that blocks out all men—the good as well as the not so good. She will not easily or openly convey her needs; she will claim, either verbally or behaviorally, that she does not need the companionship of her male partner; she will doubt his ability to understand her or her needs; and she will question his competence to adequately nurture her soul. While this type of response seems reasonable immediately after an unpleasant relationship experience, to hold on to these sentiments for any length of time is nothing less than pathological.

Articulating your needs for another's emotional support should not, by any means, be perceived as a weakness. Rather, it is among a person's greatest strength. Being able to acknowledge your assets as well as your liabilities symbolizes strength in who you are. It should be seen as an indication of the SBW's healthy perception of herself as a human being, and her ability to adapt to her environment. It says that she is able to identify complementary assets in her mate, and is resourceful enough to use them to her benefit as well as the benefit of the relationship.

While it is not the intent of any portion of this book to point fingers or assign blame, it is especially crucial that his portion not be misconstrued as making one person responsible for another person's behavior. Rather, this chapter, like previous ones, should be an exercise in perspective taking. It should become a mechanism for encouraging vigorous work on the part of both partners to support the development and growth of intimacy and emotional adaptiveness in their relationships. The SBW is in no way responsible for a partner who is defiling the relationship with behaviors that corrode trust or betray confidences. She is not responsible for a partner who treats the relationship like a competition; she is not responsible for the adulterer or the liar. She is, however, responsible, and fully so, for her role in the dynamics of the relationship.

She is responsible for making her needs known. I fully encourage women to open up to their intimate partners in a manner that is honest and engaging. I would go so far as to recommend that the SBW allow her partner access to her soul. Since you've chosen to embark upon a legally and presumably spiritually binding relationship, it would seem prudent that you would be willing to give it everything in order to achieve growth. After all, isn't that the very least that you expect from your mate? Adaptive relationships are reciprocal undertakings. It would make sense that you would be willing to give at least what you expect to receive from your partner.

To this end, it is imperative, first and foremost, that you tear down those ridiculous brick walls and take off that cape. These seemingly impenetrable facades of toughness and independence aren't shielding you from hurt. The only thing they're protecting is an illusion of total self sufficiency. None of us, no matter how many degrees we've been awarded or how much money we earn, are without need of intimacy and connectedness. No matter how many mountains we move in a day, we all need to go home to that listening ear who will relish in our triumphs and console us in the face of challenge. About the only purpose that brick wall you've constructed around you serves is to prevent you from fully engaging with your partner in an emotionally adaptive give-and-take relationship. The wall and the cape are, too often, the primary barriers in most SBW's quest for true intimacy in their relationships. They serve little other purpose than to keep you miserable and operating at a level far less than what your true emotional potential can be.

It is incumbent upon you to allow yourself to walk before your intimate partner in spiritual and emotional nakedness. Remember, superwoman doesn't have to be super, she just has to be a woman.

AFTERWORD

With knowledge comes responsibility. The wisdom imparted here comes from a place of genuine caring, concern and a sense of responsibility to my own. We've overcome battles much bigger than this, yet this issue haunts us like the ghost of slavery itself. The African American woman is the culture. She is the bearer of our children; the source of wisdom; the healer of wounds, physical and emotional. Her unceasing efforts to bring about positive change in our homes and communities in the face of every type of adversity imaginable is nothing less than heroic. She is, without question, a cultural treasure—a gem whose radiance we should admire and aspire to emulate. She should be revered, honored, and most of all, nurtured.

Even superwoman needs to cry sometimes.

SELECTED READINGS ON THE TOPICS DISCUSSED

Abraham, W. T., Cramer, R. E., Fernandez, A. M., & Mahler, E. (2001). Infidelity, race, and: An evolutionary perspective on asymmetries in subjective distress to violations of trust. *Current Psychology*, 20 (4), p. 337.

Author Unknown (1998). Infidelity: Why men cheat. *Ebony*, 54 (1), p. 116.

Baisden, M. (1995). *Never Satisfied: How & Why Men Cheat.* Katy, TX: Legacy Publishing.

Cose, E. (2002). *The Envy of the World: On Being A Black Man In America.* New York: PocketBooks (A Division of Simon & Schuster).

Cose, E. (2003). The black gender gap: Black women are making historic strides on campuses and in the workplace. But professional progress is making them rethink old notions of race, class, and romance. *Newsweek*, (March 3, 2003) p. 46

Hefner, D. (2004). Where the boys aren't: The decline of Black males in colleges and universities has sociologists and educators concerned about the future of the African American community. *Black Issues in Higher Education*, 2 (9), p. 70.

Hopson, D. P. & Hopson, D. S. (1995). *Friends, Lovers and Soulmates: A Guide to Better Relationships Between Black Men and Women.* New York: Simon & Schuster Adult Publishing Group

Lynn, R. (2002). Why do Black American males earn less than Black American women? An examination of four hypotheses. *The Journal of Social, Political and Economic Studies,* 27 (3), p. 307.

Mathes, E. W. (2005). Relationship between short-term sexual strategies and sexual jealousy. *Psychological Reports,* 96 (1), p. 29.

Maton, K. Il, Hrabowski, F. E., III, & Greif, G. L. (1998). Preparing the way: A qualitative study of high-achieving African American males and the role of the family. *American Journal of Community Psychology,* 26 (4), p. 639.

The author encourages your feedback. Please forward comments and/or questions regarding this book or its contents to: hann-morrison@earthlink.net